Bleached by Moonlight

This book belongs to:

_____

_____

Cover art by Jean Claude Roy
jcroy.com

Bleached
by
Moonlight

Poems
by
Sheena M. Roberts

◆ FriesenPress

One Printers Way
Altona, MB R0G 0B0
Canada

www.friesenpress.com

ISBN
978-1-03-831201-3 (Hardcover)
978-1-03-831200-6 (Paperback)
978-1-03-831202-0 (eBook)

1. POE000000   Poetry

Distributed to the trade by The Ingram Book Company

To
Brian for his knowledge
Steph for her expertise
Jean Claude for the cover art

*"Memories return,
bleached by moonlight,
revealing the magic
that is forever."*

(from "Broken Destiny," page 15)

Contents

Chapter Three ~ Poems for Reflection

Chapter Four ~ Poems for Fun

Chapter Five ~ Poems of the Seasons

Chapter Six ~ Poems of Immobility

Chapter Seven ~ Poems about Music

Chapter Eight ~ Poems in Motion

Poems
of
Life

Chapter One

Life

Once upon a time life was predictable, linear.
I drew the days around me
like bedcovers on a chilly night,
reality left outdoors.
Nothing disturbed the ordered sanctity
of my curled-up world

Between covers of well-worn books,
my imagination soared on wings unseen
to a Camelot reborn.
Little rocked the towering ramparts
of my castled days.

Adventures carefully navigated,
life's stages passed.
A fairytale existence with no fairy tale,
knights without shining armour,
castles with no fiery dragons.
A heroine in waiting.

Until one day the dream awoke
to find the story being written,
complete with battles and heroes dying.
Bedcovers flung aside, ramparts bridged,
a heroine unrehearsed,
left standing center stage.

Curtain final, applause silent,
with dream's desires in full retreat,
I crawl back to my bedlinen world
and begin to write.

Blue

Blue is the colour of water and sky,
of turquoise and aqua-green hues.
Caribbean days and Bermudian nights,
horizons of soft hazy blue.

I sail on a ship through an indigo night,
past a moon glowing alabaster blue.
Over cornflower clouds towards midnight I float,
wrapped in bright sapphire dreams to come true.

In the hour before dawn when the world is asleep,
in a landscape of shadowy clues,
a cobalt cathedral with spire to the clouds
rises up in the deep velvet blue.

Morning dawns clear, twinkling stars disappear,
skies are a periwinkle blue.
My dreams on delay as my ship sails away,
life awaits, I have so much to do.

But I still want to daydream
in blue.

Broken Destiny

Fragile, fleeting,
forever lost to time.
A brief flowering,
enchanting, enchanted,
now faded and gone.

Shattered faith, broken dreams,
destiny left dangling
on a rope of promises.
A single cry across
an ocean of eternities.

Between pages of life and death,
words disappear into silence.
Thoughts surface
and are embraced by the sun.

Alone, at peace,
the heart sings in duet.
Memories return,
bleached by moonlight,
revealing the magic
that is forever.

Reasons

Tempting is the path cut short,
sirenlike its call.
What might-have-been in haloed light,
pride before a fall.

Reasons for the seasons,
no small comfort, quotes unfair.
Should not springtime reign forever,
why must winter bring despair?

Wisdoms gained, acceptance feigned,
reality ajar.
Backward glances, lingering chances,
beckon from afar.

Ahead cocoons and gilded cages,
restless wanderings.
Stifled nights of smothering dark,
revived rememberings.

Mercifully, Time's passages
let youthful thoughts recede.
Glimpses caught in ember's glow
to hearth and home concede.

Sleepless

Fractured nights of sleepless bedsheets,
restless tossing, mind awake.
Staring inwards, eyes unseeing,
memories cause the heart to ache.

Drifting in and out of thoughts,
darkness weighing heavily.
Padded footsteps, window open,
moonlight floods a landscaped sea.

Overhead a twinkling mass of stars,
so far away, yet near.
Sound of waves and engine hum,
Titanic moment with no fear.

Days of sailing stretch ahead
with nothing but horizons new.
Time to think, reflect, remember.
Time for memories etched in blue.

The Figure

Silent,
he stands on the
horizon of her thoughts.
Motionless, eyes intensely blue,
his face radiating a peace before unknown.
She reaches out, only to find him gone
and yet not.

For in her heart,
a space now shares
his peace.

The Valentine

The Valentine was faded
like the pictures on the wall,
its colour gone and all the edges frayed.
Yet when she held it, closed her eyes,
his face would reappear
and the memories would come alive again.

The words she knew by heart,
each one was seared into her soul
and on the fourteenth February day of every year,
she'd read again the words of love
and smiling, touch the photograph
while whispering her words of thanks to him.

As midnight chimes,
the Valentine is carefully tucked away
in a place that only she would ever know.
Then, wheelchair moments later,
grey hair brushed, she welcomes sleep,
for on the horizon of her mind, he waits for her.

The Dance

Like music box dancers on pedestals high
or snow figurines glass-enclosed,
we spin and we dance in our own little space,
intent on the steps we've composed.

Not daring to glance lest we stumble and fall,
the rest of the world kept at bay.
What could be a waltz or a smooth pas de deux,
remains solo, danced safely our way.

Until the day dawns when we waken to find
that the music has changed us within.
We reach out to find someone waiting nearby.
It is time for the Dance to begin.

Once more the world shrinks, only this time there's two,
movements match step for step, beat for beat.
Every turn, every twist, not a gesture is missed,
two bodies, one soul, now complete.

Too soon the Dance ends but in truth we remain
in the arms of the dream that was real.
The pedestal gone, new awarenesses won,
more in touch with emotions we feel.

Then like windows that open to let in the light,
whisking shadows and demons aside.
We are freed from constraints and prepared to embrace
life's adventures with arms open wide.

tryst

moonlight tender round deep pastures
silver rimmed down nightfall lanes
stardust tempted dreams surrender
ribbons silken nights sustained
daybreak kindles sleepy yearnings
sacred darkness scented dawn
newfound dreamers sunlit traces
sweet tomorrows softly yawned
dewdrop prayers send daylight treasures
sunbeam mornings sensuous streams
silent treetop peaceful landscapes
starlight twinkles sapphired dream

Moonlightenderoundeepasturesilverrimmedownightfallanestardustempteddreamsurrenderibbonsilkenightsustainedaybreakindlesleepyearningsacreddarknesscentedawnewfounddreamersunlittracesweetomorrowsoftlyyawnedewdropprayersendaylightreasuresunbeammorningsensuoustreamsilentreetopeacefullandscapestarlightwinklesapphiredrea

A Slice of Life

A slice of life,
a taste of love,
a dream played in a dream.
A time alone,
worlds apart,
closer than it seems.

Moon-filled thoughts,
sun-drenched tears,
a song within a song.
A slice of love,
a taste of life
to memories belong.

Poems
for the
Mind

Chapter Two

Haven 911

And then one day the sky falls in.

Winged shadows touch the ground,
as a moment jars an unsuspecting world.

The silence aches in answer,
hearts and doors fling open wide,
quick to comfort those found stranded on their shore.

The Rock becomes a haven
and for some a second home,
stalwart island, autumn cliffs against the seas.

To the travellers, an oasis,
pebbled beaches stretch 'til sunset,
windswept meadows, raw emotions running free.

Brief the stay but long remembered,
newfound ties will not be severed.
Open skies await, the memories will survive.

For now, their shattered world awakes
to gather up the pieces.
Sleepless eyes uncover nightmares born alive.

Meaningless the cost, precious innocence is lost,
drawing closer, hearts are touching, hope stands taller.
Light returns to haunted faces,
pain subsides but not entirely.
Leaves a legacy,
a world forever

smaller.

Freedom

Freedom wept the hostage
as he gazed beyond his cell
to a world once close
but now forever far.

Freedom cried the seagull
as he spread his wings to fly,
soaring high as if
to touch a distant star.

Freedom begged the soldier
from the trenches of the night
as his comrades fell around him
one by one.

Freedom prayed the mother
as she held his picture close,
hoping one day soon
to see her only son.

Freedom shout the children
on the final day of school
as the summer shines
forever in their eyes.

Freedom smile the graduates
with cap and gown in hand
as they stand upon the
threshold of their lives.

Freedom, such a simple word,
is used in many ways.
Spoken differently,
the message is the same.

Remove the bars, release the hostage,
let imagination soar.
Answer prayers
and bring the soldier home for good.

Let the children just be children,
share the wisdom, let them grow.
Give them confidence
to leave their neighbourhood.

Praise their courage and conviction,
help them keep each other strong.
Tell them stories
of how Camelot once stood.

Teach them freedom of expression,
put the future in their hands.
Create a world of peace
where all live as they should.

Viewpoint

A question,
several answers,
one decision spawns another,
each opinion causes others to appear.
Every move, a new position,
prove a point or change direction,
re-evaluate, ensure what's meant is clear.

Indecision
breeds frustration,
facts misspoken cause division.
Knowledge gained and skillfully used,
succeeds with ease.
Disagreements and debates,
convincing arguments restate,
twisted meanings, reprimanded to appease.

A moment
clearly listened,
full attention, pose a question.
Viewpoints argued seem much closer than before.

Resolution or solution,
compromise without dilution.
Different viewpoints can become a unity.
Minds shake hands for new tomorrows,
open paths as yet untrodden
and it all began with such
diversity.

Perspectives

Freedom
state of mind
or State

Boredom
empty thought
or plate

Kingdom
born of heart
or place

Wisdom
state of mind
or Grace

the art gallery

framed faces
eyes unseeing
stare from silent canvas

observer or observed

figures frozen
limbs lifeless
moving in mind's eye

living or brought to life

landscaped creations
or creation's illusions

a sardonic grin
a fleeting smile
merely shadow play

who is on display here

turn around and see
or be seen

Eden

If experience is wisdom
and with wisdom comes insight,
does living with eyes and ears shut
constitute blissful ignorance
or simply narrow mindedness?

If experience is opening oneself up
to the possibility of unbearable pain,
does living with one's heart tightly closed
mean that happiness is assured
at the status quo;
in the absence of extremes,
a kind of emotional entombment?

If with age comes knowledge
and knowledge brings awareness,
can higher education
create intellectual paralysis
over infinite parades of possibilities?

As charming as innocence and inexperience,
as refreshing as absence of intellectual strength,
to deliberately remain in such a state
could be viewed as an even greater tragedy.

Until one considers that
knowledge, experience and wisdom
count for little
in the absence of belief in oneself.

Closed

The closed mind is frustrating.
How does one get in
or climb out?

The closed mind is confusing:
existing without substance,
yet taking up space.

The closed mind is dangerous,
its powers universal, the after-effects insidious,
its tentacles reaching the farthest corners of civilized intellectualism
destroying kingdoms of brilliance
with one
vacant
stare

The closed mind is illusionary.
Look in a mirror and describe what you see,

if anything at all.

Ruins

Stately sentinels of a Gothic past,
arched buttresses once soaring
now crumbling with dignity.

Monuments to moments frozen in time.

Memories captured forever in stone,
echoing along silent corridors
strewn with relics of bygone rituals.

The mind wanders down cloistered hallways
darkened through years of neglect.

A shaft of sunlight illuminates
a forgotten corner and images dance
in the swirling dust beams.
Laughter-filled remnants twinkle
deep in sunken eyes then disappear.

Memories retreat
into the mists of yesterday.

Brigadoon of the mind,
guardian of the past,
keeper of the present.

A solitary figure on
the landscape of tomorrow.

Resignation

If this moment were forever,
if I stayed, could I belong,
surrender thoughts and feelings, right or wrong?
In a moment briefly frozen,
glimpse directions yet unseen,
different drummers marching to a single song?

Hold the moment,
stand in anger in defiance of the norm,
overturn the old and usher in the new.
In a moment so united,
sounding leadership alarms,
the inner sanctum closes ranks without a clue.

Will this moment be forgotten
'mid tomorrows of today,
will all questions disappear along the way?
The moment waits in silence,
sees the messenger is gone,
knows the message left behind is here to stay.

Jigsaw Puzzles

I do the edges first.

I like knowing where the boundaries are,
how big the big picture really is.

I like the enclosed feeling.

It becomes my space, I own it.
I can do whatever I want within that space.
I can do whatever part of the puzzle calls out to me.

I like the feeling of control.

I can work on the puzzle whenever I like.
I can pause indefinitely
and return another day,
another week,
next month,

or not at all.

incomplete

unexpected
unintended
ended

Poems

for

Reflection

Chapter Three

The Dragon and the Butterfly

One day a handsome dragon met a pretty butterfly.
Said the dragon, "How are you today and why are you so shy?"
Spoke the butterfly, "I'm fine and I'm not shy and who are you?
You look just like a dragon but your scales are shiny blue."

"Why yes," replied the dragon, proudly polishing his scales.
"I had the colour changed because I thought I looked too pale.
No matter how much fire I breathed when practising my roar,
it didn't feel impressive, so I needed something more."

He waited for approval but the butterfly just stared.
She'd always thought that dragons couldn't possibly feel scared.
He looked so big and handsome that her heart went flitter flop.
She blushed and turned to fly away, then heard him holler, "Stop!"

The butterfly looked back and saw the dragon hang his head.
"I'm sorry for the yell, I meant to say, please stop, instead."
He looked so sad, the butterfly responded with a smile,
"I'll stay and keep you company for just a little while."

And so began a friendship that with time turned into more.
The dragon and the butterfly each other did adore.
For then one day instead of two, they found that they were three,
and that is how the tiny dragonfly first came to be.

Praying Mantis

Have you seen a praying mantis as it sits upon a leaf,
body motionless and poised as if in prayer?
So perfectly the colour of the leaf on which it sits
that one hardly even notices it's there.

Have you seen a caterpillar as it inches on the grass,
pausing every now and then to take a bite?
So considered every movement, left alone to take its time,
hours later it is gone and out of sight.

Have you seen a tiny beetle as it crawls across the floor,
heading bravely into areas unknown?
Watch it linger, almost falter, then resume its silent quest.
What propels it to continue all alone?

Have you seen a human being as he rushes off to work,
briefcase bulging with reports complete at last?
So intent on beating traffic, cell phone held against his ear,
car horn blaring, going nowhere very fast.

Praying mantis, tiny beetle, caterpillar, all so small,
they have learned a lesson few of us will know.
In this life of destinations it's not where we have to be,
it's the journey, what we see, and how we go.

Why

Ask a seedling why it sprouted,
where it came from, how it grew,
ask a snowflake why it melts upon the ground.
Ask a river where it wanders,
when it stops or how it sleeps,
ask a raindrop how it falls without a sound.

In this world are many wonders,
many questions without answers,
nature's miracles exist since time began.
Watch the seedling in the sunlight,
touch the snowflake softly falling,
feel the raindrop as it lands upon your hand.

Take all of Nature's wonders
and enclose them in your heart.
Save them up for dreary days when work is done.
Take them out and let the miracles
renew your faith in living.
Put them back and step once more into the sun.

Curve Balls

In the middle of a hectic pace,
life throws us curve balls.

Meant to bring us up short,
they catapult us out of our treadmill routines,
putting a spin on an otherwise linear existence.

In slowing down we find ourselves examining:
the web before the spider,
brush strokes before the painting,
hearing silences between words,
glimpsing fleeting expressions
of changing moods.

Time takes on a different meaning.

As the body heals, any challenge
becomes an arduous task.
Wheelchair accessible is merely
an indicator of the size of an obstacle,
not its absence.

Then joyously, we are back.
Hamsters on ever-spinning wheels.
We stride with confidence into our future,
blinkers slipping unnoticed back into place.

However, we have missed the most important
lesson of all.

In always anticipating what might be,
we often fail to fully appreciate what is.

Avoidance

I want to make a difference
but I fear I'm losing me.
I shuffle thoughts and dreams around
amid a paper sea.

Outside the days grow longer
as the winter turns to spring.
Yet stubbornly I stay inside
and to my tasks I cling.

I claim to have a purpose
that my goals to me are clear.
But I know that avoidance
is, in truth, the issue here.

My life is what it is,
how I change it is the key.
Delay will only grow
a paper ocean from the sea.

The Path

Begun in youthful innocence
oblivious to any plan,
centered on friends and family
we grow as best we can.

From baby steps to adulthood
experience helps us all
to choose the right direction,
tho' now and then we fall.

At times it all seems clearer
then suddenly we're lost.
The path has changed direction
and not without a cost.

Recovery is painful,
the lessons learned are real.
We're older, hopefully wiser,
more in tune with how we feel.

We carry on and as the days
grow shorter we can see,
that life was never meant for those
who need a guarantee.

For looking back we realize
the path was always there.
Just hidden in the future,
silent answer to our prayers.

children

honesty of expression
openness of thought

freely forgiving
willing to be taught

bluntness of opinion
charming in their talk

readily accepting

can we walk their walk

Easy

It is easy to live in a world
where you are sure of the things you know.
If you know a lot,
you can confuse those who don't.

It is easy to ask and then decide
that the answer is not what it should be.
If you are loud enough,
most will bow to your assumed knowledge.

It is easy to build a wall to protect yourself
from arrows that pierce your heart.
If you keep the wall high enough,
not even you can get out.

It is easy to say you don't want out,
that you do not need the world outside.

If you stop looking over the walls,
you will never know who might be there.

Living Life

Living for oneself is lonely.
Living inside a comfort zone is isolating and numbing.

Step outside the box and step into life.
Step outside the comfort zone
and face a world that is

frighteningly vibrant,
confusingly convincing,
maddeningly wonderful,
and more-ish.

March to the beat of your own drum,
but don't let it drown out the rest of the band.

Take time for yourself
but not the same time every day, every week.

Make promises to yourself
but be ready to break them should someone need you.

In short
be prepared to let go
of yourself

Answers

If you're looking for a rainbow
without waiting for the rain,
if you're building lofty castles in the air,
if your thoughts can't seem to focus
on the tasks you've set before you
and your mind keeps running circles everywhere.

If outside the winds are calling you
to chase the clouds 'til sunset,
if the trees are swaying, offering limbs to climb,
if nature has a hold of you
and tempts you with her beauty,
if the days are long but leave you with no time.

If the plans you make keep changing
in direction without warning,
if your dreams keep disappearing out of sight,
if your heart is saying something else
is waiting 'round the corner,
if your prayers are left unanswered every night.

If life insists on turning like a carousel forever,
'til you wish that it would stop for just a while.
Close your eyes, think of good times
and the people closest to you
and the memories are bound to make you smile.

Then turn your focus inward,
dig down deep as deep you can,
sit in silence, simply listen, calm your fears.
Find the strength that lies within you,
strength that waits to be discovered,
never quit and soon the answers will appear.

Poems
for
Fun

Chapter Four

Classical Mice

Classical mice
(at a bargaining price)
but a word of advice,
they're not very nice
when munching on rice.

Classical mice
(at a very low price)
like playing with dice,
eat bread by the slice
over cocktails on ice.

Classical mice
(at a giveaway price)
are friendly with lice.

So never think twice,
buy a trapping device.

Classical mice

Free!

The Begonia

I bought a huge begonia
and set it in the hall.
My friends all said, it won't grow there,
it has no light at all.

My begonia doesn't know this,
it seems to like its place.
It keeps on growing taller,
now I fear it needs more space.

The words were barely out when
from the hall there came a crash.
I raced downstairs to find that
all the china had been smashed.

My plant was stretched across the hall
and underneath a door.
It had grabbed the china cabinet
and pulled it to the floor.

I stared around in horror
and was just about to cry,
when I caught a glimpse of something
out the corner of my eye.

The begonia was shaking,
I could almost hear its glee.
Instead of feeling badly
it was making fun of me.

I turned around to speak
but the begonia was gone.
I found it curled around a pot,
its mischief finally done.

The moral of the story is,
no matter how content,
do not believe your garden plants
have innocent intent.

Evolution

It used to be that men would hunt
while women stayed at home,
to clean the cave
and keep the children fed.

When day was done the men returned
with wildebeest in tow
and promptly dragged
their women off to bed.

Now if the female species
had protested way back then,
to gain respect
and also more control.

They could have changed their diet
and turned vegetarian
and cut their hair,
so husbands had no hold.

Ode to a Chocolate

O sweetest square of deepest hue,
you sit so innocently.
Upon my desk your squareness rests
as you look up at me.

Of all the chocolates I have known
you are the perfect size.
One bite is all to start the fall
and hasten your demise.

Perhaps I should have mercy
and allow you to remain
a few more days, in many ways
it would be more humane.

To leave you sad and all alone
with nothing left to do
but contemplate impending fate
would not be fair to you.

So goodbye chocolate, farewell friend!
You will not suffer long.
Don't get a fright, I will not bite,
one gulp and you are

gone.

The Defenceless Dentist

I can't abide a toothless bride!
the dentist cried,
my hands were tied!

You know I tried to look inside,
I even said, please open wide.

But when she jabbed me in the side
I almost lost it and replied,
how dare you!

Then I sighed and lied
as upside down my face she eyed.

How dare you think you could decide
to drive alone, you could collide.
So let me offer you a ride."

I thought I'd take it all in stride
'til she convincingly implied
that I could for us both provide.

Speechless I thought not to chide
but Jekyll-like turned into Hyde.

The only choice, (as an aside),
was clear,

it must be pesticide.

Poems

There's a poem in the hallway,
there's a poem in the shed.
There are poems in the bedroom,
some are dancing in my head.

There's a poem in the kitchen,
I saw it on the sill.
I politely said please go away.
I do not think it will.

There's a poem in the bathroom,
I saw it in the sink.
There's another in the closet,
why it's there, I cannot think.

I am trying to ignore them
and I hope they'll disappear
but they seem to be all over
and I fear they like it here.

So, can someone, if you hear me,
tell my family that I've found
another place that has more space,
where poems are not around.

The constant need to rhyme
can often muddle up the brain.
So I'll return when I can write
non-rhyming poems once more.

The Yellow Song

When I woke up this morning,
the sun was shining bright,
the smiley stickers on my bed
were grinning in delight.

For breakfast the bananas
sang in four-part harmony,
while eggs yolks winked
from beds of white
and grapefruit smiled with glee.

Along the kitchen counter
lemons boogied in the sun,
as macaroni pieces
marched behind them one by one.

Outside the dandelions
asked the daffodils to play.
The bumblebees hummed merrily
as buds began to sway.

The sunflowers waved to buttercups
and golden rod sneezed back,
while yellow peppers tangoed out
and down the railway track.

With cobs of corn and margarine
lined up to sing-along,
above the noisy merriment
rose echoes of their song.

On with my sou'wester,
yellow wellies shiny new,
it's time for an adventure,
come along, there's room for two.

We'll travel in a school bus
down that famous yellow road,
munching popcorn made with butter,
singing loudly as we go.

It's a yellow kind of day today,
let's all stand up and shout!
Yellow is for happy times,
that's what our song's about.

When you feel down,
just put on yellow clothes and you will see,
your sunshine will return to you
and with it, harmony.

The Bear with No Hair

There once was a bear
who was born without a hair.
He wore a big bandana
so the people wouldn't stare.
Then one day he was sittin' in his chair,
when up on his head there grew a big hair.

Now the bear with the hair
couldn't wait 'til he could share.
He bowed his head so everyone
could see that it was there.
Then one day when he looked, he had a pair,
with more growing all over
goodness knows where!

Now the bear with the hair is normal as can be.
He plays and eats and runs around
each day like you and me.
He knows that someday when he's old
he'll lose the hair he sees.
'Til then he'll be the bear they call,

The Great Grizzly.

The Puffin Patrol

We're the Puffin Patrol, comic and droll,
with our masks and our bright-coloured beaks.
In tunnels below, our families grow,
so you often won't see them for weeks.

We're the Puffin Patrol, not quite in control,
our take-offs and landings lack style.
We dive for our fish, find the tastiest dish,
then stop to digest for a while.

We're the Puffin Patrol, quite the busiest souls,
walking on webbed-orange feet.
Though our comical face makes us seem out of place,
we're the cutest of birds you will meet.

The Mouse Pres

There's a far-away island (least everyone says)
where a piano mouse came to be pres.
This mouse wasn't famous or clever or tough,
(it played the piano and practised enough).

But this tiny grey mouse had a talent you see,
it thought up ideas, not just two or three.
It thought up a dozen or more in one go
and out they'd all come like a volcano blow.

Just how they began was a lot like sneeze,
with a tickle back deep in its mind.
Then growing and growing till out of control,
the "kerchoo" was quite one of a kind.

At first these explosions were such a surprise
that its friends stood there frozen in fear.
'Til the look in its eyes
let them soon recognize
when a "sneeze" was about to appear.

They tried different methods to stifle the sneeze
and control the kerchoo when it came.
But they could not succeed,
'twas annoying indeed,
for results came out always the same.

'Til one day they had a terrific idea,
they made the mouse pres of them all
and sat it up high
on a throne in the sky
so ideas would spew out and fall.

Now the islanders walk with umbrellas held high
and ideas bounce onto the floor.
If someone has need,
they take what they see
for the mouse pres keeps sending down more.

Being Four

Now you're four you can't ignore
the fact you'll have not just one chore,
but chores galore and even more!

Now then, can you close the door
and pick your toys up off the floor
and put your clothes back in the drawer?

Oh no, you'll cry: But why? What for?
I'd rather be in bed and snore,
or buy some Lego at the store.

I'd like to try a lion's roar
and build a plane to watch it soar,
or take my sword to fight a war,

'cause that's what
being four
is for.

Poems
of the
Seasons

Chapter Five

Spring in Newfoundland

Bright skies glitter
over frosty-white landscapes.

Chilly north winds blow
down evergreen valleys,
across frozen ponds.

Final sweep of Sheila's Brush.

Hours later, snow patches visibly shrinking,
skies are a hazy grey.

A robin hops across his melting kingdom.
Crocus tips push bravely up
through sodden ground.

Fog tendrils drift in over coastal hills
then snake along winding streets.

April in Newfoundland.
Best kind.

September Night

Twinkling harbour, silent streets,
windstill treetops, echoing feet.
Fragrant leaves in rustling grass,
moonlight crescent,
full moon past.

Summer nights soon growing long,
midnight walks around the pond.
Shadowed lamp posts,
random thought,
webs in time forever caught.

Leaf Cycle

A
leaf
hangs
tenaciously
past its season.
Sun-scorched, limp, wind-whipped,
buffeted by dancing breezes.
Refusing release.
The other leaves flutter gently in downward spirals,
pirouetting daintily or tumbling,
twisting in mocking dives.
Flashes of bold brilliance,
boastful,
are
g
o
n
e

Then one night, alone, the leaf executes a triple pirouette
and smiling softly, curls up in the arms of the waiting earth.

Dark Moon

Dark moon, scudding clouds,
wet leaves plastered to rainslick roads.
Street lights wink,
bright eyes blink.
Windswept visions in minor modes.

Haunted moon, pumpkin round,
memories sacred pierce the sky.
Nightfall rhythm,
windowed prism.
Rainswept gutters riding high.

Faded moon, early dawn,
misty threads on gold-tipped trees.
Bird calls start,
sings the heart.
Sunswept moments in major keys.

A Christmas Moment

Looking up, a twilight sky,
crescent moon hung low.
Buildings sit, windows lit
with lights, a Christmas show.

No wind, no rain, the pavement bare,
all traffic noises still.
A moment clear, one almost hears
a whisper: peace, goodwill.

Standing there, the eyes reflect
the magic of the scene.
A moment blessed, the senses rest,
knowing what it means.

No price to pay, no layaway,
one only has to pause.
A gift for free, for all to see,
no tree or Santa Claus.

Moments special, magical,
appear and then are gone.
But left to be, these memories
will linger all year long.

a little piece of Christmas

snowflakes falling on your nose
a little piece of Christmas

moonlight footprints, frozen toes
a little piece of Christmas

laughter echoes through the trees
warming heart and soul

midnight walks and quiet talks
a little piece of Christmas

Song at Christmas

Starlight dancing, reindeer prancing,
dreams of moonlight cross the sky.
Street lights blinking,
treetops winking,
silent night songs drifting by.

Snowflakes falling, voices calling,
wishes festive fill the air.
Late night yawning,
new day dawning,
bedtime footsteps on the stair.

Stories ending, prayers ascending,
thoughts of morning tucked away.
Church bells ringing,
anthems singing,
Joy to all this Christmas Day.

Advent Thoughts

Hope, Peace, Joy and Love
the Advent candles gleam,
reflected in the shining faces
soon to sleep and dream.

The world is set to celebrate
the wonder of a birth,
yet not all hearts can dance this night
for some, there is no mirth.

Behind the mirrors of their eyes
lie pools of hurt and pain
that glistening tinsel, lights and trees
can never quite explain.

The youth that bravely saunter by,
bravado in their stare,
belie a burden we can't know
nor they will ever share.

The forms that lie in alleyways
away from neon lights,
are there for reasons long forgot,
they've given up the fight.

Look past the lights and tinsel,
listen just beyond the hum.
Hear a world that will not change its speed
to match another's drum.

The challenge is in the doing.
Some people stand and say
the kinds of thoughts that stir the mind,
then sweep them all away.

Instead of words, take action,
instead of soon, choose now.
For Advent thoughts and wishes
can become a Christmas vow.

Snow Angels

Memories.
Unforgettable.
Nights when snowfall lies fresh,
sparkling under white-masked street lights.
Towering walls lining pristine roads,
dwarfing snow-drenched houses.
Snow angel nights.
Heaped mounds inviting
laughter and snowball fights.

Collapsing into deep drifts,
half-buried in white blanket layers, giggling, hiccuping,
heads back, we stretch out arms and legs to make snow angels,
large, deep-winged snow angels

Gazing up into the frosty heavens,
cold seeping through garment layers,
we roll out of our molds, declare a winner,
and fling ourselves once more into fresh banks of white,
snow-suited specks adrift in an arctic whiteout.
Looking up through snow-crusted lashes,
we lie in the hushed silence,
the sky staring back.

Then, evening church bells ringing in our ears,
we topple to our feet
and head home
to hot chocolate dreams.
Magic!

Christmas-ing

Frosty tingling, voices mingling,
Christmas-jingling night.
Pine trees twinkling,
paper crinkling,
snowflake-sprinkling sight.

Midnight ringing, carol singing,
stars are shining bright.
Faces beaming,
eyes a-gleaming,
wondering at the light.

Log fire blazing, children gazing,
warming thoughts held tight.
Voices praising,
love amazing,
all is feeling right.

Cattle lowing, hearts a-glowing,
Christmas time is past.
Prayers ascending,
never ending,
Peace on Earth at last.

Christmas Lights

Coloured lights and decorations may be fine,
but there are those whose hands will never light a tree.
It's not easy to remember when the world is all a-glow,
that for some a room with empty walls
is all they'll ever know.

When Christmas song surrounds us with its cheer,
think of those whose ears will never hear.
Eyes that cannot see the snow fall, feet that cannot dance,
feeling life has passed them by,
not given them a chance.

But we can be the hands that light their trees,
tell them of a world they cannot see,
hold their hands and help them feel the rhythm of a song,
take them out beyond their walls,
and show them they belong.

If we take the time to listen and to share,
we'll find a world we never really knew.
Then the magic of that Christmas long ago will come again,
A lesson of the season,
reaching hearts since time began:

Christmas lights are brightest when they light up what's within.

Christmas Past

Memories of Christmas past.

Early morning giggles
and forbidden exploring, whispered warnings
and smothered sounds of retreat.

Then silence,
bursting into squeals of laughter
as bodies torpedo themselves under covers,
cold toes meeting bare skin,
erupting into a writhing sea of blankets.
Momentary truce.
Heads pop up in impish delight
and the chase begins anew.

From the hallway, approaching footsteps
herald the festive frenzy.
Dancing figures scamper downstairs to sit,
wiggling with excitement.
The adults smile,
surveying the chaotic scene, anticipating each body lunge,
smoothing tangled hair, welcoming chubby hugs
and sticky I love you's.

A peace settles.
Tired bodies lie in carpeted heaps,
eyelids drooping, hands still attempting to play,
every now and then a quiet hiccup.

Memories of Christmas past.
Visions of Christmas today.

After Christmas in Newfoundland

The tinsel droops, the garlands hang
more crooked than before,
the tree lights flicker shadows 'round the room.
Wrapping paper lies in shreds
mid tangled ribbon tails
while the fireplace sputters softly in the gloom.

From down the hall float voices,
sounds of music, mirth and song,
with bursts of laughter, toasts and rowdy cheers.
The doorbell rings to no response,
more bundled shapes pile in,
just as welcome here at Christmas as all year.

With mummers, kitchen parties,
always something on the stove,
Christmas spirit reigns supreme
with room to share.

The celebrations last until
Old Christmas Day is past.
But the warmth of heart and hearth remain
to bring our Island Rock the fame
for hospitality beyond compare.

Poems
of
Immobility

Chapter Six

confined

dawn trembles
born on a breath

I waken
to muted daylight
dust motes dancing
along frayed curtain edges

motionless shadows
mocking my inert form
stretched beneath
layers of pain

I wait in vain for relief

perhaps tomorrow

abdicated

the body has abdicated
thrown down its crown
refusing to move as it should

someone ought to inform it
that this is not right
this is not how the game is played

the term of office is for life
there is no successor waiting in the wings

its return is required immediately
come back now

please

outburst

my pot has boiled over

my patience and positivity
have had a tantrum
I am temporarily undone

excuse me while I wallow in self pity
I will pull myself together
in a moment

there
outburst finished
I am back

comparison

my pain is small
not life-threatening
no need for hospitalization

it will not last but is enough
to make me crave a little sympathy
a word or two of support

I do not need to hear about your pain
at least not right now
all I require is
a moment of understanding
for my pain

thank you
now
how are you doing

Recovery

A pain-free moment,
the next day more,
a spasm passes, I grin.

Two more steps, not a twinge,
not a twitch, not a cramp.
Is the healing about to begin?

I straighten my shoulders,
look out through the door
to the kitchen and hallway with stairs.

Can I do it? Of course!
Not too fast but not slow.
If I stumble and falter, who cares!

I can't wait forever, life has to go on,
nothing ever gets done sitting still.

So, challenge accepted.
Look out, here I come.
I can do it, I must,
and I will!

Early Onset

An ache, nothing more,
vaguely disturbing yet explainable.

For now.

Until the pain crescendos.
Then the twitch.

The first outward sign that the body
has abdicated responsibility.
Still, no need for concern.
Daily routines drown out any fears.

Keep moving.

Instinctively the body adapts,
hides, camouflages,
while inside a war is waged,
the winner already declared,
scales tipped years ago.

Facts unalterable.

But the mind refuses facts,
preferring hope.

Life continues, changes subtly.
Nature's way of softening
the blow.

rollercoaster

to lose track of oneself

to come and go
on the whim of chemicals

is this a disability
or a cruel joke

one minute able to do everything
the next minute

not

The Visit Home

He stands beside the sleeping form
intent, and holds her hand.
Motionless, he feels her pulse
then sits, he understands.

The tie between them keeps them strong,
but now it's growing clear,
the pain and pills erode the will,
the end may soon be near.

They've made their peace, are not afraid,
they know Who waits above.
For this is but an ending only
of their earthly love.

As daughter who has lived away
and built a life apart,
to see a parent trapped in bed
is too much for the heart.

I say goodbye and turn to leave
not knowing if I'll see
them both together once again,
for that's not up to me.

The sky awaits, the ground below
soon disappears from view.
My life is back where I belong
with all I have to do.

The past stands on the threshold of
a future yet unknown.
Whatever happens, I am glad
I made the visit home.

Requiem

Golden light floods
the late afternoon landscape.
Fingered shadows creep
across furrowed fields.
Cottages huddle isolated,
subdued, guarded.

An engine shudders to life,
shattering the silence.
Lights flash hypnotic circles
then disappear from view.
Time to leave,
time to grieve.

Emotions in turmoil,
bodies exhausted,
minds in shock.
A final glance,
then eyes forward.
Unbelieving.
Unbelievable.

Anguish succumbs
to velvet anonymity.
Restless sleep
awaits the dawn.
The heavens lighten,
bird calls begin.

Pheasants strut their ritual,
hares zigzag in play.
Strips of bright yellow tape
shine garishly,
then droop, as if to say
this is enough,
let the healing begin.

Release

At heaven's gate the angels wait
for one more weary soul.

With folded wings they softly sing
of love that makes us whole.

If with grief comes true belief
from pain there is release.

As time goes by the tears will dry
the heart will find its peace.

Poems
about
Music

Chapter Seven

The Piano

Silent now, once the ivory keys rang
through parlour windows, over rosebush gardens.
Youthful sonatinas chasing stately minuets
down tree-lined crescent walks.
Scales dancing merrily around stern etudes
before fading with time.

Children gone, grandchildren a continent away,
a figure sits, silver haired, hunched in years.
Gnarled fingers tentatively
seeking forgotten melodies,
thin voice remembering the distant past.

The keys reply, warmed by the wandering touch,
patiently rewarding each
rediscovered note with a velvet sound.
Together they lose themselves in duets and songs
from another time and place.

Past blurs with the present and alone again, lid open,
the piano begs silently to the empty room.
Sighs of wooden creaks go unnoticed.
A shimmer of chords ring out hopefully as a duster
flicks unceremoniously over the keys.

Then finally, oh sweet rapture, young fingers touch,
hesitant, exploring with growing exuberance.
Notes cascade in uninhibited play.
Sonatinas and minuets tumble out
from under flying fingers.
The piano laughs with glee, and is reborn.

piano lessons

I watch
and listen with awe
and wonder

in all reality
who is the teacher here

The Recital

Head bent, eyes intent,
fingers poised to play.
Quietly there, with tousled hair
his body starts to sway.

Parted lips, suspenders slip,
totally unaware.
A tiny grin, time to begin
he wiggles on the chair.

Barely begun, piece is done,
he scrambles down to bow.
With tie askew, he grins anew
runs safely off, somehow.

Years fly past, a graduate at last,
he strides upon the stage.
With bearded chin, but still the grin,
a pianist come of age.

A final pause then huge applause
acknowledged with a smile.
Eyes a-glow, he turns to go,
a musician now with style.

Says goodbye and in mind's eye,
he leaves but not alone.
For following near, a figure clear,
the boy has never gone.

Music Camp

Yawning doors greet early morning faces,
instruments slung low from sleepy shoulders.
Bleary eyes beneath tousled hair
focus in vain on dancing black dots.

By mid-morning a cacophony of brass and woodwind
mingle with percussive shots
as figures dart in and out of classrooms.

Amidst the chaos a tall figure strides down the hall
with petite campers in duckling file,
past a cavernous gym where rows of dancers
rehearse in synchronized steps.

Minutes later a wheelchair inches out of a doorway
then accelerates, followed by a flock
of giggling keyboard players.

Mischievous faces gaze back innocently
at lunchtime reprimands
and sidle out of forbidden territory.

By late afternoon energy levels are subsiding.
Tired figures head home with instruments in tow.

Once again the building sits silent,
darkness blanketing the windowed shape,
as it waits patiently for the music
to bring it back to life.

Weekend Jam Session

Slamming of doors, spirited voices
shatter the Sunday silence.
The studio is transformed
by a tangle of bodies and instruments.

Rooms ricochet with laughter.
Gleaming black pianos wait impatiently,
power chords snaking underfoot.

An unseen signal and the cacophony
stammers to a brief halt then resumes.
Heads bent, eyes locked, hands in rhythm.
The enthusiasm is infectious.

Spontaneous musical combustion.

Music transcending time and space,
where there is no past,
only present.

The Dangers of Practising Piano

My teacher says that practising's not dangerous at all,
but I found out today that she is wrong.
I've bruises on my elbow, cuts and scratches on my hand,
and all because I tried to play my song.

I ran into a wrong note, played a left hand chord too soon,
my fingering got tangled in a mess.
I lost my place completely when I couldn't hear the tune,
so the only way to finish was to guess.

My eyes were red from staring at the notes upon the page,
the kitchen clock said just five minutes more.
My music fell, I bumped my head and knocked the metronome.
It smacked me as it fell onto the floor.

So now I have to count out loud, it's got me so confused,
I can't remember what I have to read.
I'm tired of repetitions 'cause they're putting me to sleep,
and glissandos make my finger knuckles bleed.

If practising's not dangerous, then where did I go wrong?
Perhaps I need to change the way I play,
I've only had one lesson and not practised very much,
so I guess I'll wait and try another day.

A Spook-tacular Practice

Welcome, dear students, come in if you dare,
we may look unfriendly, but really we care
about how you practise, and so to be fair
we thought we'd explain that you'd better beware!

When you sit down to practise, don't mind if we stare.
To succeed under pressure is really quite rare.
We know how important it is to prepare.
Without proper testing you won't have a prayer.

This new way of learning with you we will share,
play any wrong note and we'll give you a scare.
After your practice take time to compare.
You'll find the mistakes will be simply not there.

Don't thank us, we're happy to help clear the air
and show that your music can have quite a flair.
When practising notes with no bars to repair,
your work will be over with minutes to spare.

Just one word of warning, don't dance on your chair,
lest careless mistakes creep back in unaware.
Practising badly will cause such despair,
for loss of perfection
is your worst nightmare.

Musical Mayhem

There's trouble with the Treble
and the Bass is out of line.
The Tenor's throwing tantrums
while the Alto sits and whines.

The Staff is at a meeting,
they forgot to leave the Key.
The Tonic Notes are homeless
and have lost their Melody.

The Bars are out of order
and the Notes can't find the Beat.
They've gone to take a Rest
and will return with the Repeat.

The Meter has been changed,
all the Eighth Notes are not pleased.
They used to come in two's,
now they have to group in three's.

The Double Bar has been delayed,
Dal Segno was misread.
Its shortcut sign was overlooked,
Da Capo done instead.

Now Fine is upset because
the music's ending late.
All sixteen bars must be replayed
instead of only eight.

The tune has been restarted,
the end is very near.
Conductor signals, last note sounds,
applause and encore cheers.

The Impossible Bar

To play the impossible bar,
to learn an unlearnable song,
to count with incredible patience,
correct any notes that are wrong.

To fix an unfixable tune,
to hear every nuance of sound,
to play as if all were perfection,
avoid the mistakes that were found.

This is my quest, to practise that bar,
no matter how tricky, or even bizarre,
to play every note without stumble or pause,
to be ready to walk on the stage
and receive the applause.

And I know if I conquer this bar,
put myself to the test,
I'll feel proud, and I know I will show
that I've practised my best.

How I play will be better for this,
can't give up after coming so far.
All I need is to practise more hours
and repeat the impossible bar.

intention

to sit at the piano
self aside .
keys resisting touch

centering
emptying the mind
of all that limits

listening
beyond
the printed page

sensing
the spaces
between the notes

ready to play
behind the sound where
the essence of the music resides

waiting
for the music
to begin

Lisztian Encounter

The piano crouches,
lid open, keys exposed,
passionate, ferocious.
A lisztian tiger
waiting to be tamed.

The first chord sounds,
demands submission.

The music retreats into a corner
lashing out with the occasional sf.

Then, surrendering to silence,
subdued, inarticulate,
the piano sleeps
until the next encounter.

Poems
in
Motion

Chapter Eight

Departure

Sleek shapes crouch patiently
in the early morning darkness,
motors rumbling,
outstretched wingtips twinkling
through swirling fog.

Rows of tiny windows reflect
the sheen of jet-black tarmac
as figures scurry antlike below.

More delays,
then the first tentative nudge.
Unceremoniously inching backwards,
the endless lumbering across
mazes of runways begins.

One last sweeping turn,
engines crescendo
to a shuddering release.

Anticipating freedom,
the runway races below.
A final thrust and airborne.

Nose to the heavens, heading upward
into the blue space of silence.

Beauty in motion.
Poetry in flight.

Night Flight

Freed from earthly constraints,
suspended over sea-foam clouds,
the imagination soars and time stands still
as we race towards a shell-pink morning,
flashing wingtips motionless against the night sky.

Cabin lights are dimmed to the sound of engine drone.
Movie screen images flicker over rows of blanketed figures,
asleep, except for one solitary passenger.

Wide awake, face pressed to the window,
watchful eyes widen in wonder
as below, a break in the carpet of clouds
reveals the twinkling lights of a slumbering city.

Minutes later, the twinkling city
disappears behind a bank of clouds,
leaving behind a memory of a brief
but magical encounter.

soaring

gracefully gliding
flying free
high in the heavens
I long to be

soaring in silence
swooping low
buffeted by breezes
to and fro

teasing the treetops
heading high
catching an updraft
to the sky

floating in freefall
ridges rush by
nose tip to touchdown
I love to fly!

The Cruise

On a northbound summer evening,
a cruise ship slips through an Alaskan sunset.
Voices, music, midnight minstrels,
elegant timelessness.

Narrow channels peppered with islands
widen to majestic scapes,
cry of whales echoing
down icy corridors of eternal silence.

On a southbound afternoon,
the cruise ship dwarfs a sleepy coastal town.
Wind, water, throbbing engines,
rugged peacefulness.

Helicopters buzz overhead
like giant bumblebees,
dipping in mock display
before disappearing in scattered formation.

On a homeport morning,
an airplane rises into the blue, sunlit haze.
Talk, thoughts, fractured feelings,
solitary sadness.

Below a shimmering expanse
of seascape memories
and sunswept decks,
jazz at five and evening promenades.

For some an end, for others just the beginning.

Seniors' Prom

Shiny bowties, dancing shoes
tux and polished pates,
with eager eyes and beating hearts,
they scan the room for dates.

A week at sea and single women
never wait for long.
The band begins and soon the floor
reflects the dancing throng.

Waltzes, rumbas, foxtrot moves,
cha cha cha's and spins,
unabashed they tango past
with youthful smiles and grins.

Studied moves to ballroom twirls,
awkward steps to glides,
passengers of the twilight years
have nothing left to hide.

Midnight chimes, reluctantly
the dance floor starts to clear
and cabin bound they head,
the music ringing in their ears.

For those who think the Senior Prom
is it, then they think wrong.
For seniors that are young at heart
still dance to any song.

tactility

polyester rhythms,
satin tangos in the dark
chiffon waltzes
'round the fountain
denim rhumbas through the park

flannel foxtrots past the fireplace
velvet sambas, tartan reels
cotton polkas
sequinned ragtime
weaving senses sound and feel

Black

shining black
impatient hooves
nostrils flaring
as he moves

twitching ears
velvet eyes
reins resisting
as he shies

turning circles
stubborn change
sideways moving
shakes his mane

nudging nose
playful shove
dark coat gleaming
groomed with love

swinging head
shining sun
pasture waiting
lesson done

Shooting for the Moon

Rakish pose, impish grin,
questions, answers
tumbling in free fall.
Imagination on a rollercoaster ride
of vibrant hairpin turns.

Motion in music, music in motion,
eyes alert, insistent.
Conversation belies
the months and years dedicated to
turning the switch back on.

Frustration erupts.
Thunderclouds threaten then vanish
as mind and body fling themselves
gleefully into the next moment
and another page is turned.

For those who know,
the past is a miracle
and each new day,
a celebration.

Playground at Midnight

Night settles over a sleeping city.
Beneath shadowy limbs,
shapes frozen in eerie play.
Midnight mist muffles distant traffic,
Echoes of daytime swirl in the damp air.
A playground oasis.

Suddenly the darkness erupts
as a lean figure
races down a path to the swings
and in seconds is airborne.
A whoop of exhilaration
as toes touch treetop leaves
on their way to the moon.

Energy spent, swing dangling,
silence lies heavy in the air.
The young adult pauses
on the edge of the playground,
one foot on the sand, the other on the path.

Swings twist tantalizing,
slides yawn, bars beckon.

Lingering,
reluctant to go,
Peter Pan existence tempting,
his eyes scan the shrouded shapes,
then turning, leaves childhood voices behind.

On Becoming a Poet

Emotions raging, grief unabated,
prowling a cage of forever.
Words appear, born out of unseen depths.

Release, then peace.

Life returns,
a kaleidoscope of normalcy.
The spark is gone, the need subsides.

The true test begins.

Craftsmanship,
the creative mind self-ignites,
spins beauty and horror
from nothing.

Poet.
Perhaps.

The honeymoon is over.
The proof lies
in the absence of need.

My Favourite Poems

Title   Page

_____

_____

_____

_____

_____

_____

_____

_____

My Favourite Poems

Title   Page

_____

_____

_____

_____

_____

_____

_____

_____

_____